Also by Mike O'Mary

The Note

A story about the power of appreciation

Wise Men and Other Stories

by Mike O'Mary

Dream of Things
Chicago, Illinois
dreamofthings.com

Copyright © 2009 by Mike O'Mary

All rights reserved. No part of this publication may be reproduced or transmitted in any form or by any means, electronic or mechanical, including photocopy, recording, or any information storage and retrieval system, without permission in writing from the publisher.

Published by:
Dream of Things
Chicago, Illinois
dreamofthings.com

ISBN 978-0-982-57941-1

First Dream of Things Edition
December 2009

Dedicated, with love, to my mother, Barbara

Many

of these

essays were

first read on

WNIJ - Northern

Illinois Public Radio,

as part of NPR's *Morning*

Edition program. Others were

published, sometimes in different

versions, in the following publications:

Chicago Tribune Sunday Magazine, Peoria

Journal Star, Denver Post, Rocky Mountain News,

Baltimore Sun Magazine, Cleveland Plain Dealer, Detroit

Free Press Sunday Magazine, Louisville Courier Journal,

Joliet Herald, and

Catholic Digest.

Contents

Wise Men 3
Snow Ice Cream 9
Unwrapping Our Gifts 13
The Scariest Costume 19
Decorating the House 23
John's Thanksgiving 27
The Best Meals 33
Christmas at the Carl Sandburg Mall 37
The Christmas Program 41
Family Men 49
Kid Talk 55
A Note From My Sister 61
The EcoSphere 67
Little Arms 71
Holiday Parties 75
The Difference Between Men and Women 79
New Year's Resolutions 83
The Rose Parade 87
The Top Ten 93
The Scrabble Tournament 97
Dog Days 111
Lucky Duck 115
Heaven 127

Wise Men and Other Stories

by Mike O'Mary

Wise Men

When I was in the second grade, I played one of the three wise men in the St. Elizabeth of Hungary Christmas play. I was the second wise man—the one that brought the frankincense.

I enjoyed being one of the wise men. It was a pretty easy part. The first wise man says, "We are the three wise men. I bring you gold," and that serves as the cue for the next wise man who says, "and I bring you frankincense," and so on.

We also got to wear robes. I brought a bathrobe from home.

But the main thing was that you were a "wise man." There were bigger parts—Mary and Joseph had pretty substantial roles, and even the innkeeper and shepherds had more lines—but being a wise man was quite a distinction. You had to carry yourself with grace and dignity. You had to look wise.

That's why I was a little confused when I learned that Mike Walston had also been designated a wise man.

Mike Walston was the poor kid of the class. As it turned out, most of us at my old school were pretty poor, but we had not yet seen enough of the world to know it. What we did know was that we were better off than Mike Walston.

We knew because we started each day at St. Elizabeth's by going around the room and telling Sister Julia what we ate for breakfast that morning. It turned out that Mike Walston seldom had breakfast. When it was his turn to answer, he'd stand up and smile a big unselfconscious smile and say, "Nothing." After the kids laughed at his answer a few times, he stopped smiling, but his answer didn't change. As it was, Mike Walston was singled out as different, possibly ignorant, and, generally speaking, not a good person to associate with. All I knew was that the honor of being designated a wise man had been diminished by my having to share that distinction with Mike Walston. And to make matters worse, he was the head wise man. He was to present the gold.

We began rehearsals right after Thanksgiving. We three kings would stand in the wings during most of rehearsal, Mike Walston first, me behind him, and Joey Amback, the myrrh guy, behind me. When it was time for us to enter, Mike Walston, being gold, would lead the way.

Unfortunately, Mike Walston was having trouble remembering his lines. ("We are the three wise men. I bring you gold.") And, of course, every time he stumbled during rehearsal, the class would laugh at him. I only made matters worse by making faces whenever he messed up, causing the class to laugh even louder.

As we got closer to opening night, Mike Walston was still having trouble. Many of us speculated that Sister Julia would have to make a switch, and that I, being frankincense and the next wise man on the totem pole, was the likely candidate to move up. So when Sister Julia asked me to stay after school the day before the performance, I was prepared: if she felt my talents were better suited to the role of head wise man, I would, with all due grace and dignity, accept the promotion and present gold to the Christ child on opening night.

But that's not what Sister Julia wanted. Instead, I heard these shocking words: "I want you to help Mike Walston remember his lines when we perform the play tomorrow night."

I couldn't believe what I was hearing.

"I want you to practice his lines with him before you go on stage," Sister Julia continued, "and if he forgets his lines when he kneels down by the baby Jesus, I want you to kneel down beside him and whisper his lines to him so the audience won't know he forgot."

I said I would do it.

Sister Julia dismissed me, and I walked home that day in a daze. This was not the way it was supposed to be. Nonetheless, the next night, I did as Sister Julia told me. Mike Walston, Joey Amback and I showed up in our bathrobes, somebody from the props department handed us cardboard crowns covered with tinfoil, and then Mike Walston and I went right to work on his lines: "We are the three wise men. I bring you gold."

He did it fine offstage when he was relaxed, but I was afraid that once we got on stage, he'd freeze. I was prepared though: if he froze,

I'd kneel down beside him and bail him out. If nothing else, my friends would know who was the hero and who was the goat.

The play went on and we watched as the innkeeper turned Joseph and Mary away, they shacked up in the manger, and the sheep and goats and cows gathered around. Mike Walston and I went over his lines once more while the shepherds did their thing, then it was time for our big entrance.

Mike Walston led us across the stage toward the Star of Bethlehem and the manger. With Mary and Joseph looking on, Mike knelt in front of the baby Jesus and—didn't say a word. He froze. I was about to kneel down to help him, but just then, he glanced up at me and smiled a big smile. Then he turned, looked at Mary, and spat out his lines in the same matter-of-fact tone he used when he told us about breakfast: "We are the three wise men. I bring you gold."

I was stunned. There was a fairly long pause before Joey Amback gave me a nudge. Then I remembered where I was. I knelt down next to Mike Walston, turned to Mary, and said, "And I bring you gold."

I couldn't believe my own words. I was the frankincense guy, but I had said, plain as day, "I bring you gold." There was a shocked hush over the entire church basement audience—broken only by a few nervous coughs—until Joey Amback knelt next to me and said, "Yeah, I bring you gold, too."

Then the whole audience roared. The third wise man had bailed me out. Life in the second grade would go on. I would not have to spend my remaining days standing against the fence during recess. And Mike Walston would receive kudos for his fine performance.

The lesson stuck with me. Years later, when my boss was having trouble and there was talk of replacing him, I remembered the Christmas play and lent him a hand. Sure, I wanted to move up, but not at all costs. There's room for compassion in this world. I know firsthand that the wisest of wise men stumble once in a while. And when that happens, it's nice to have somebody around who will cover your rear.

Snow Ice Cream

The first snowfall. When I was little, new snow meant one thing: we'd get to make snow ice cream.

As soon as enough snow had accumulated on the ground, my mother would send my brothers and sisters and me out to collect the new snow in mixing bowls, drinking glasses, soup cans—anything we could find. Then we'd bring all of the containers back to the kitchen.

While Mom dumped the snow into a big glass mixing bowl, we kids would take off our coats, hats and gloves, and spread them throughout the rest of the house to dry over any available furnace vent. Then we gathered in the kitchen where we'd take turns warming our feet over the vent next to the oven.

Mom would take the big bowl of snow, add some sugar, milk and vanilla extract, and mix it all up. Then she gave us each a bowl full, and we sat around the kitchen table—me with my little brothers and sisters at a time before we were old enough to know pain or worry—eating snow ice cream while Mom took care of everything else.

Those were rare, beautiful moments…frozen in time, frozen in memory…and I'd give anything to go back to that kitchen with my mother, brothers and sisters for just five minutes.

I haven't had snow ice cream in a lot of years. And there are probably many reasons not to eat snow ice cream nowadays. Even though new fallen snow may look pure and white, there are probably lots of impurities in the stuff. It's just a matter of time before somebody sounds the alarm about the harmful effects of acid snow.

Even so, snow ice cream still sounds pretty good to me. It sounds like kids warming their cold little toes over the furnace vent. It sounds like Mom mixing up a batch of something cold and sweet in the kitchen. And in the middle of shopping for presents, sending out Christmas cards, decorating the tree, balancing the checkbook and myriad other holiday-related activities, it sounds like a pretty good way to spend a December afternoon.

Where do we keep those mixing bowls anyway?

Unwrapping Our Gifts

When we open our presents at Christmas, I am in charge of gathering up the wrapping paper.

I don't know exactly when or why I became my family's designated cleaner-upper, but over the years, as I've gotten to know myself a little bit better, I understand that this was no accident. Getting rid of the wrapping paper is part of who I am.

I learned from my mother how to wrap gifts. She wrapped things in plain white tissue paper with a simple ribbon and hand-made bow. And after all the presents had been opened, she gathered up the tissue paper, ribbons and bows, and saved them to be used again next year.

After witnessing her simple and efficient methods for years, I was amazed to learn how much effort some people put into wrapping Christmas presents.

Don't get me wrong. I don't fault people who go to the time and trouble to wrap a gift nicely. Many people even have their gifts wrapped right at the department store—which is the way I would do it if money were no object. You could accuse them of being lazy or of wasting money, but the way I see it, they're supporting all those gift wrappers working in all those gift-wrapping departments for the holiday season. There's nothing wrong with that.

But we do need to keep things in perspective. I think we all agree that when it comes to gifts, it is the thought that counts. And the gift wrap—being once removed from the gift, and twice removed from the thought—should actually matter nary at all.

So that's why I'm out there getting rid of the paper as soon as it comes off the gift. I figure the fewer distractions there are, the more likely we are to get down to the important things: the good feelings between the person receiving a gift and the person giving it.

If I could, I'd even get rid of the gifts. But I've been told I will be barred from all future family functions if I start hauling away presents as soon as they've been opened.

One of my friends is always telling me, "I'll hold a strong thought for you." That's what I want under my tree. In a perfect world, we'd remove the wrapping paper and find strong thoughts from all our friends and relatives. And when I stop and think about it, that's exactly what I get.

But still, every once in a while, the thought gets lost in the Christmas shuffle. That's why I think it would be nice if we could do away with the gift-wrap and the presents. Then we could all sit around the tree on Christmas morning and share our thoughts of each other.

But most of us can't quite bring ourselves to do that. The kids probably wouldn't understand that kind of Christmas as well as they understand a Barbie Christmas or a Wii Christmas. And there's something to be said for the joy of giving.

It's the pros and cons of issues like this that make me think life is not so much wonderful as it is ambiguous. Fortunately, wonder and ambiguity are not mutually exclusive.

I myself would probably not be very good at sitting around a tree telling people how I feel about them. I suspect many people are the same way. That's why we enjoy giving presents. If we can't tell them how we feel, we can at least try to show them with a little gift at Christmas.

And if you've really neglected someone throughout the year, you can get them a big gift at Christmas. Retailers love guilt.

We are funny creatures. We usually know what's important, but those things seem so weighty and imposing that we are easily distracted. We go bowling when we know in our hearts and souls that we should be spending time with our children. Or we don't go bowling when we know in our hearts and souls that we need time to relax and be with friends. I think it was Aristophanes who first said that many of life's mysteries would be solved if there were only some magic formula to accurately determine whether it is the right time or the wrong time in one's life to go bowling.

And, of course, we spend lots of money on big Christmas presents when all most people want is to know that they are loved.

Anyway, I said it was no accident that I ended up being the one in my family to gather up the wrapping paper at Christmas. I've spent a lot of time in my life trying to find the right balance between the package and the contents—between the things we regard as distractions and the things we consider to hold meaning.

Along the way, I've known a number of people who have spent the better part of their lives focusing on their own personal gift-wrap instead. Appearance is everything. They wrap themselves up without realizing that many people would be more interested in what's inside.

And I've known yet another group of people who have spent their lives stripping the distractions away. These people are best described as "focused." They figure out what they want to do with their lives and they focus on that, refusing to be sidetracked. They have found their gifts, but they sometimes forget to share them.

As with most things, the answer probably lies in moderation. It's true that too many distractions can prevent us from realizing who and what we are—from being aware. But in keeping with life's ambiguity, it's those same distractions that give life its rich texture. We don't need to become hermits, but in everything we do, we need to try to find what's important.

I have an inkling of what's important at Christmas. And since I can't strip away the gifts, the least I can do is get the wrapping paper out of the way.

Here's wishing you an Uncluttered Christmas and a Very Ambiguous New Year.

The Scariest Costume

I'm going to a costume party this weekend, and I don't know what to wear. I'm not very creative, so I'm thinking of going as my evil twin. Or I might go as an Olympic water polo player. Something about me in a Speedo and a bathing cap strikes me as funny. It could also be pretty scary.

If I really wanted to scare people, I'd go as a midlife crisis. The dictionary defines it as "a period of emotional turmoil characterized by a strong desire for change." A professor I once had defined it as the death of your father.

I haven't reached a midlife crisis yet, but I hear footsteps. And when I turn around to see what's coming, I see myself, way back there—so far back that I may never catch up. So far back, I'm almost gone.

In between are lots of people that sort of look like me. There's me the father and me the son. Me the husband, brother, son-in-law, and my old friend, me the soccer coach. Me the student, the writer, the foreman, the public relations guy…you get the idea. Sometimes I look back and wonder what happened to that other guy. Is there anything left of him or is he gone forever? It's frightening.

I think this happens to a lot of people. We go through life taking on various roles, and if we're not careful, we lose track of ourselves. Before you know it, people are saying, "What happened to him? He used to be so much fun." Meanwhile, you wander around, fulfilling your duties, but with a vague sense of disillusionment. Then your father dies, and next thing you know, you're headed for the beach in a convertible with a woman half your age while your wife and kids sit around waiting for the child support checks.

I don't want that to happen to me—except maybe for the convertible part. So I think I know what I'm going to do for this costume party. I'm going to go as myself. I just hope somebody recognizes me.

Decorating the House

Last weekend, I put up the Christmas lights at our house. My greatest fear is of falling off the ladder while I'm decorating. I know I've got to go sometime, but I want it to be in a blaze of glory: foiling a band of terrorists by taking a bullet for Santa at the mall...stopping a herd of stampeding reindeer in order to save a sleigh full of Christmas toys for the orphanage...something dramatic. What I don't want is to be found dangling from the downspout with a noose of burned out Christmas lights around my neck.

I can hear the kid next door now:

"Mom! Some big, fat Santa in a dirty sweat suit just hung himself."

Fortunately, his mother will be there to comfort him: "That's not Santa, stupid. That's Mr. O'Mary. Now get back in here and practice your Nintendo."

This year, I have a new problem: something has been eating the lights I put around the bushes. My daughter thinks it's a rabid raccoon. The neighbor kid thinks it's an alien that eats electricity.

I think it's the new guy who lives in the condo down the street. He used to work as a geek in the carnival. When the carnival came to our town last summer, he said, "This is it. I'm home!" Ever since then, decorative lights have been disappearing.

Tonight, I'm going to stand guard, and it occurs to me that this may be how I go out: defending the Christmas decorations from a light bulb-eating carnival freak. But more likely, you'll be able hear the neighbor kid yelling, "Mom, some big, fat Santa in camouflage pants is being eaten by a rabid raccoon!"

And his mom will say, "That's not Santa. That's Mr. O'Mary—and my, doesn't his house look festive!"

John's Thanksgiving

My best friend, John, will probably be mad at me for telling this story. But it's such a great Thanksgiving story, I can't resist. Forgive me, John.

This happened many years ago, during John's first year of college. He had gone East from Idaho in order to attend a prestigious university. And now that his first school vacation—the Thanksgiving holiday—was at hand, he had decided to remain out East rather than travel back to Idaho to be with his family. He had some friends at school, but most of them had gone home for the holidays.

So come Thanksgiving Day, John woke up in a deserted dormitory building. That in itself would be enough to depress many people. Waking up alone on Thanksgiving Day. But he got up, got dressed and was doing fine. Until he called home to talk to his family members, all of whom were congregated at his parents' home for a big turkey day feast.

One by one, John talked to everybody at his parents' house.

"They were all having a great time," said John. "I could imagine them sitting in the house warmed by the wood stove...the Salmon River and the Sawtooth Mountains off in the background...the perfect Thanksgiving Day setting. And there I was, talking on a pay phone in an empty dormitory 2,000 miles away."

I envisioned John talking to his mother who, of course, missed him terribly and wished he had come home for Thanksgiving. John's older brother, often the aloof intellectual, had come home for Thanksgiving, and he, too, said that he would miss John at the dinner table. Then John talked to a steady procession of aunts, uncles and family friends. All were having a good time—and all told John he should have come home.

All the while, John could hear the sounds of the holidays in the background. The nonstop hubbub of multiple conversations taking place simultaneously. The excited rise in pitch whenever another guest or relative arrived. The collective exclamation when the turkey was removed from the oven.

Finally, John talked to his father who had just returned from the traditional Thanksgiving Day pheasant hunt. His father probably said something to him like, "Missed you on the shoot, boy."

John got through the phone conversation, got himself dressed in jacket and tie, and bravely went out for his turkey dinner at a nice restaurant near the university. But between the phone call and sitting alone at the restaurant, he found himself getting very depressed.

Fortunately, just a couple of tables away, there was an elderly couple. They were also having dinner alone. They saw John sitting by himself and invited him to join them for Thanksgiving dinner.

Unfortunately, John declined.

"That was so stupid," he says now. "There I was, all alone at Thanksgiving, missing my parents, and there was this nice couple—probably with a kid in college somewhere who couldn't be with them for the holidays—and they were nice enough to invite me to have dinner with them. And I was too stupid to accept."

After that, John was so self-conscious that he rushed through his turkey dinner. He even skipped dessert so he could get out of the restaurant as quickly as possible. Instead, he stopped on the way back to his dormitory and bought a frozen pumpkin pie and a quart of Cool Whip.

When he got back to his room, he scarfed down all of the pie and whipped cream in less than ten minutes. When he was finished, he was so bloated, tired and emotionally exhausted that he practically passed out in his bed—empty pie pan at his side—and slept through the rest of Thanksgiving Day.

"It was the worst Thanksgiving I ever had," he says. But don't feel too sorry for John. He gets lots of sympathy from anybody who will listen to his grim holiday tale. My wife and I, for example, were so moved by this tale of pathos, that we made a special Thanksgiving dinner for him when he visited last year—and it was only October! He won't fess up, but I'm sure he's parlayed his story into similar sympathy meals many times over.

But the real bright spot of this story is, of course, the nice elderly couple. They tried to do the right thing. And even though it didn't work out that time, they are to be lauded.

It takes courage to reach across the gulf that separates one human being from another. We revel in our individuality, but there are times—and Thanksgiving is one such time—when we should be with other people to celebrate the things we have in common: occasional loneliness, yes; but also compassion, humor, an appreciation of beauty, and a once a year hankering for hot turkey and cold cranberry sauce.

So the next time somebody asks you to join them for dinner, think seriously about accepting. And if you are doing the asking—and if you happen to be asking a self-conscious young college student from Idaho—please persist.

The Best Meals

What was the best meal you ever had? The topic comes up every year at Thanksgiving at our place. After we've consumed another meal seemingly beyond compare, I invite friends and relatives to draw comparisons.

The best meals don't necessarily hinge on the food. Some meals are special because you earn them. In July 1987, after two days of strenuous hiking in the Sawtooth Mountains with my friend, John, I ended up at the Rember Ranch in Stanley, Idaho, where Betty Rember made a sourdough pancake dinner that I will never forget.

Some meals are special because of the company. In August 1974, I went camping with three buddies from my old neighborhood. We were only 18, but the way we talked about the "good old days," you would have thought we were in our eighties. That weekend, we feasted on catfish filets, fresh-baked bread and bean soup that had simmered for 24 hours—all courtesy of Tom Mudd's grandfather, who packed a meal for us when he learned all we were taking was hot dogs and RC Cola.

But the best meal I ever had was in November 1983 in Genoa, Illinois. A group of friends and I drove from Galesburg to Rockford to see Eric Clapton in concert. Afterwards, it was too late to drive all the way home, so one of our party, Rick Foote, directed us to his grandparents' house in Genoa.

It was a modest home even by Genoa standards, and we arrived unannounced well after midnight. But Rick's grandparents welcomed us with open arms and made beds for each of us.

The next morning, my friends and I got up at dawn thinking we should leave before we wore out our welcome. But Rick's grandmother beat us to the punch. The kitchen table was already set, and she served up bacon, eggs, pancakes, syrup, sausage, homemade biscuits, gravy, hash browns, toast, butter, jam, coffee, milk and fresh-squeezed orange juice. It was a feast fit for kings, let alone bumbling college students.

It was obvious that Rick's grandparents were not wealthy people, yet they held nothing back. It was only after we repeatedly insisted that we couldn't eat another bite that Rick's grandmother finally sat down to rest.

I've never forgotten that meal. I realized at the time that it was being prepared out of a grandmother's unwavering love for her grandson. I just happened to be in the right place at the right time to share in it.

I think of that meal every year at Thanksgiving because I learned that the key ingredient to the best meals is not something you find in a cookbook or a recipe. No, the key ingredient comes from somewhere else. It comes from the heart of the person preparing the meal.

When the chef brings unwavering love to the table, every meal is a feast.

Christmas at the Carl Sandburg Mall

December 1977. Galesburg, Illinois. I wasn't doing very well in college. The academic affairs committee suggested that I take some time off. At first I declined their offer, but they politely informed me that if I didn't take some time off voluntarily, they would make the decision for me. All of a sudden, a little time off didn't sound so bad. I soon found myself looking for a job at the Carl Sandburg Mall, out near the freeway bypass on the north edge of town.

The Carl Sandburg Mall. What would he say if he were alive today? (The fog comes/on little cat feet./It sits looking over the Carl Sandburg Mall/shudders in revulsion/and then moves on.)

I applied at nearly every store in the Carl Sandburg Mall before Jim Jurinak, the manager at the Shoe Inn, a division of the giant Shoe Corporation of America, called me in for an interview. "You could manage your own store if you catch on quick," he told me.

I told him I was interested—my career options were limited at the time—and he hired me on the spot.

Selling shoes is not the worst job in the world. Especially at Christmas. People are buying gifts. They pick out a style, tell you a size, and if you have it in stock, they buy it.

The unpleasant part was that the Shoe Corporation of America insisted that a certain percentage of each employee's sales be in accessories—shoe polish, socks, purses, etc. Apparently, shoe companies make more money on polish and socks and purses than they do on shoes—which makes you wonder why they don't dispense with the shoes altogether and just open up a sock and polish store.

Anyway, it turned out that I was not very good at selling polish and socks and purses. My career in shoe sales was soon in jeopardy. Eventually, Ted, the district sales manager from Peoria, came up to evaluate my performance for himself.

He visited on a busy Saturday morning. Jim Jurinak and Ted went out to a bench in the Carl Sandburg Mall to talk. Things got busy. I kept waiting for the two ace salesmen to come in and help, but they never left their bench. I ended up waiting on all the customers. Later, when Ted left and Jim Jurinak returned to the store, I asked him why they hadn't come in to help me.

"We wanted to see how you would handle a rush," said Jim Jurinak.

"How did I do?" I asked.

"Some people just aren't cut out for the shoe game," said Jim.

It can now be told that I never actually had any interest in the shoe game or in managing my own shoe store. But I couldn't quite tell Jim Jurinak that back then. I wish I could have. It would have saved us both a lot of trouble. Instead, I expressed my heartfelt desire to succeed at shoe sales (at least until I could get back in school), and Jim Jurinak had pity: he agreed to teach me the intricacies of the shoe game.

I held that job for almost a year. During that time, I watched Jim Jurinak closely. I also learned the lingo: "Six pack of tube socks with those sneakers, Ma'am?" and "Need any mink oil today?" and "We have a lovely macramé purse to go with those sandals." Along the way, I also shared Jim Jurinak's humiliation every time he tried to demonstrate the proper way to sell accessories—only to be turned down.

I eventually went back to school, but I've often thought of opening a shoe store as a retreat for people who could use a lesson in humility. Imagine your favorite corrupt politician trudging back to the storeroom with a stack of shoe boxes after blowing another sale. Or a sharp-dressed televangelist groveling at your sweaty feet, praying for a pair of Odor Eaters. Or a self-indulgent pop star answering to the district manager for not selling enough suede cleaner. A lot of people would benefit from a little humility, and there's nothing more humbling than trying to peddle mink oil at the Carl Sandburg Mall at Christmas.

The Christmas Program

My daughter's day care center was to have a Christmas program the Friday afternoon before Christmas. All of the little kids, ages two through four, would gather on stage in the center's gymnasium to sing Christmas carols for us proud parents.

In the weeks leading up to the program, my wife and I got a pretty good inkling of what songs were to be sung that day. Our daughter rehearsed constantly, and although she was sometimes off key and occasionally skewered the lyrics, she put us more in the holiday spirit than any Bing Crosby album could have.

My wife and I both made plans to attend the program that afternoon. We are fortunate in that we both work for employers who understand the importance of such events. We are also fortunate in that we live in a small town and could each be at the day care center ten minutes after leaving work.

Unfortunately, the afternoon of the program, a rather wet, icy snow was falling. It wasn't too bad, but it was enough to turn my ten minute drive into twenty. By the time I finally got to the day care center, every parking space was taken. I parked a couple of blocks away and ran through the falling snow to the gymnasium.

Fortunately, my wife was already there and had saved a seat for me. A short while later, the kids came out. Their faces lit up with smiles as they looked around the gymnasium and saw their parents and grandparents.

Then they went into the program, which consisted of "Jingle Bells," "Rudolph the Red Nosed Reindeer," "Oh Christmas Tree" and "We Wish You a Merry Christmas." I took a few pictures during the program, but then I noticed that about a dozen other parents were taking photos and shooting video. I have nothing against video cameras or photographs, but we sometimes spend so much time and energy trying to capture the moment on film, that we forget to enjoy the moment itself. So after a while, I put my camera down and just listened to my daughter and the rest of the kids sing. Nothing compares to the singing voices of four-year-olds. It was a peaceful interlude to the hectic holiday season.

After the program, the kids marched off the same way they had entered—single file, one class room at a time—then we met back in their rooms for cookies and juice and a visit from Santa. It was quite a big time for the kids—and for the adults.

When all was done, my wife had to go back to work, so I took my daughter with me to go home. I also took my daughter's bag full of "stuff"—her blanket, her teddy bear, and various holiday arts and crafts she had constructed in class throughout the holiday season. I had my hands full, but we bundled up for the hike to the car and headed out into what had now become a blinding snow storm. It was a long cold two blocks to the car, but we knew once we got there, we would be able to head straight for the warmth of home.

At least that was the plan—until we got to the car and discovered my keys were missing. I searched every pocket quickly and somewhat frantically (I was standing outside in a blowing, wet snow with a cold little girl at my side), but to no avail. Then I remembered that I had jogged the two blocks to the school. My keys must have fallen out of my coat pocket along the way.

So there we were in the blowing snow. We couldn't get in the car because I had locked the doors. I could have walked home had I been by myself (the cold, wet snow and wind hitting my face would have been suitable penance for losing my keys), but this was no weather for a four-year-old. Besides, we would not have been able to get into the house once we got there—when I lost the car keys, I also lost the house keys.

I took a quick look in the immediate vicinity of the car hoping to find the keys on the ground, but no such luck. So I picked up my now whimpering daughter and hiked the two blocks back to the school, all the while watching the ground for keys. Unfortunately, in the hour since I had jogged from my car to the gym, about three inches of snow had fallen. No keys were to be found.

Back at the school, I searched my daughter's classroom and looked around in the gym. Still no keys. They were outside, buried somewhere in the ever-deepening snow. There was nothing to do but to wait until my wife got off work and could come pick us up.

I made a call to my wife to let her know what had happened. It would take her a while to drive back across town in the snow storm, so my daughter and I went to sit by the front door to wait the 20 or 30 minutes it would probably take.

It has taken me a long time to get to this point, but it's that little chunk of time—that 20 or 30 minutes—that I really wanted to tell you about.

You see, I had looked forward to my daughter's Christmas program, hoping and expecting that it would be something special—and it was special—how could it not be? I know enough to realize that most things only happen once in a lifetime, and this would be the only time my four-year-old daughter would sing Christmas carols at a day care center with 20 other four-year-olds. But up to that point, it had been a little too rushed and a little too hectic—too many flash bulbs flashing and video cameras whirring. It wasn't until I lost my keys and my day was forcibly brought to a screeching halt that I got this reprieve…this quiet moment in which I found myself sitting cross-legged on the floor by the front door of the school, spending a few moments with my daughter.

We talked about school and snow and Christmas, and when we were done talking, I got a bonus: my daughter gave me an encore performance of her Christmas program. If there is anything more beautiful than a choir of four-year-old voices, it's a four-year-old singing a capella.

While we sat there, we also got to watch the comings and goings of various other people. I saw a number of parents coming to pick up their kids. These were parents who for one reason or another had not been able to come to the program that afternoon, and as each one passed by, I was reminded how fortunate I was to have been able to see the Christmas program.

As the kids filed out one by one with their parents, the day-care teachers also bundled up and prepared to venture out into the snow storm. I seldom said more than hello to anyone other than Miss Adele and Miss Kelly, the two women who took care of my daughter's class. But even though I didn't know any of the other teachers very well, not a single one passed without asking what was wrong. And upon hearing the saga of the lost keys, each teacher in turn offered us a ride home. I politely explained that my wife was on the way, and with that, each teacher wished us a merry Christmas, smiled and headed out into the cold.

When my wife finally got there, my daughter and I got our coats on, grabbed all our stuff, and then ran out to the nice warm car. On the way home, we stopped and used my wife's extra keys to get my car and drive it home.

Overall, we were slightly inconvenienced, but in retrospect, I feel the lost keys were a blessing. The gym full of preschoolers singing Christmas carols was special in and of itself, but I had the added pleasure of sitting alone with my daughter for half an hour...of listening to her sing Christmas carols while nice people came and went...of learning that so many people were willing to help us when we were stranded...and of doing all of this knowing that there was someone out there who cared enough about us to leave work on a moment's notice to come and get us in a snow storm.

I wouldn't wish lost car keys on anybody—especially not in a snow storm. But sometimes it takes something like that to make you slow down and count your blessings.

Postscript: A week later, the weather turned unseasonably warm and the snow melted, so my daughter and I walked over to the day care center to look for my keys. Four-year-olds are good at finding things, probably because they're closer to the ground. And sure enough, my daughter found my keys. Another blessing? Luck? Either way, I was a pretty happy guy.

Family Men

Over the last few years, I have been fortunate enough to get to know a man named Bud Toohey.

Bud's real name is Clarence. His friends call him "Bud." To his family, he is simply "Pop."

I like Bud because he is a family man. We need more family men.

Bud came of age at a good time. The Great Depression was over. World War II had not yet started. He met and married a beautiful Penn State graduate named Kay, and the young couple settled down near Meadville in northwest Pennsylvania.

Bud did not have a lot of money, but he borrowed enough to start his own business. He turned out to be a very good businessman. During the 1940s and 1950s, he built up a profitable tool and die company. He and Kay also had two beautiful daughters along the way. Things were going well for Bud.

Over the years, Bud provided well for his family. He gave them a good home, took them on vacations, made sure they were fed and clothed and well educated.

He was also able to do the things he liked to do—including attending Shriner conventions and playing golf. He eventually sent both his daughters off to Slippery Rock State Teachers College where they each met young men. That's when things started going wrong for Bud. (Or so he thought at the time.)

The first inkling that things were not going his way occurred when Bud's oldest daughter, Kathleen, brought home a cocky young athlete named Jerry.

Now I must acknowledge up front that, in Bud's opinion, very few young men, if any, would have been good enough for his daughter. And this Jerry kid had a number of marks against him to boot.

First of all, Jerry was Catholic. Bud and his family were Methodists and, on a more personal level, Bud just plain hated Catholics.

Second, Jerry was of eastern European stock—Czech to be exact—and while Bud had nothing in particular against eastern Europeans, he had always assumed that if he had to see the Toohey girls marry, it would at least be to fine Irish lads.

Finally, though not a millionaire, Bud was fairly well-to-do by this time. Neither Jerry nor his family had much money, and the thought may have crossed Bud's mind that the kid had an eye on Bud's money.

Despite these strikes against him, Jerry let it be known that he intended to marry Kathleen. Bud was appalled, and throughout the entire courtship of his daughter by this upstart kid, Bud never showed any sign of acceptance or approval. Which only made Jerry that much more determined. Finally, without Bud's approval or acceptance, Jerry married Kathleen. Bud might have softened his stance and accepted his new son-in-law after a reasonable grieving period, but the arrival of a baby girl slightly less than nine months later only convinced Bud that his new son-in-law was no good.

Family lore has it that Bud did not speak to Jerry for the next three or four years. During that time, Jerry and Kathleen had two more children—two boys—and family lore also has it that, were it not for the exceptional beauty and grace of that first baby girl, Bud might have had nothing at all to do with Jerry or Kathleen.

Bud's other daughter, Sheila, did not fare any better in Bud's eyes. She also met her husband, Larry, at Slippery Rock. Also a Catholic. Also eastern European (Polish). Sheila and Larry married a few years after Kathleen and Jerry.

None of this made Bud very happy, but gradually, he began to accept things as they were. He came to enjoy the company of his daughters again. He liked his grandchildren, too. But he could still do without his two sons-in-law.

Although it would be many years before he would greet either son-in-law with open arms, Bud saw from the start that Jerry was working hard to provide for his family—first as a school teacher, then as a restaurant manager, then as a salesman. Larry was also a hard worker. If nothing else, Bud could appreciate hard work.

Bud was impressed enough that, when he came across a good idea for a new business, he suggested it to Jerry and Larry and loaned them the money to get started.

To make a long story short, that loan paid off in spades. Jerry turned out to be an exceptional salesman, Larry ran things at the plant, and together they turned that initial loan from Bud into a multi-million dollar business.

Bud himself retired a wealthy man, but shortly after his retirement, his health began to fail. He had to give up his tool and die business. His wife, Kay, always active and capable throughout her life, took care of him at home—until she unexpectedly died of a heart attack in 1983.

After the death of Kay, Bud's daughters moved Bud to a nursing home near them. Of course, nursing homes are expensive, and Bud's money eventually ran out. But don't worry about Bud. As I said, that loan paid off. Those eastern European, Catholic boys are now taking care of Bud. Things came full circle.

Things turned out all right for Bud because although he didn't like his new sons-in-law at first, he still did the right thing: he provided for his family. And although Jerry did not like the way he was treated early on, he was not spiteful later in life.

None of this has been lost on me. In this age of easy divorce and broken homes and abandoned children, one thing is clear: Family is more important than ever. You take care of them first. No matter what.

Because Bud and Jerry knew that, things have turned out quite well for me. You see, I married Jerry's daughter. And although Jerry was not crazy about me at first, he has since gone out of his way to treat me as one of his own sons. I'd like to think it's because I'm such a great guy, but more likely, it's because he remembers how he was treated by his father-in-law.

And the story goes on. I now have a daughter. My number one goal is to take care of her. My number two goal is to let her go when she's ready to go. If I happen not to like her choice for a husband—and I must acknowledge up front that, in my opinion, very few men, if any, will be good enough for my daughter—at least I'll know how to act. I've seen two good, solid family men in action.

Bud is in his eighties now. Sometimes he forgets things. He has his good days and his bad days. He moved out of the nursing home and now lives with his nurse in a condo that Jerry and Larry bought for him.

The condo is on a golf course, and in the summer, when Jerry is playing a round of golf, he'll drop in on Bud to say hello. Bud is always glad to see him.

On one occasion, Jerry dropped in, got a cold drink and stayed to joke around with Bud for a while. They had a good time, but eventually, Jerry had to get back to his golf game.

After Jerry left, Bud turned to his nurse and asked, "Who was that kid?" Bud's nurse told him that "kid" was his son-in-law. Bud smiled and said, "He's all right."

As I said, Bud forgets things sometimes. He has his good days and his bad days. But you can bet on one thing: whenever his sons-in-law drop by these days, Bud considers it a good day.

Kid Talk

My wife needed some time to do some work one weekend, so I took my daughter to see a movie. On the way out of the theater, we ran into one of my daughter's little friends from day care. Their conversation was one of the most charming things I have ever heard.

My daughter: "Hi, Megan."

Megan: "Hi, Kathleen."

Kathleen: "I saw you watching the movie, Megan."

Megan: "I know."

They smiled at each other for a moment.

"I would like a hug," said Megan.

"Okay," said Kathleen.

They hugged.

"You're my best friend, Megan," said Kathleen.

"You're my best friend, too," said Megan.

After that, the two little friends parted ways, promising to see each other at day care the next day.

As I said, it was a perfectly charming little exchange. Sure, my rendition of the encounter sounds like the script for an episode of the Smurfs or the Care Bears, but the thing that struck me about my daughter and her friend was their sincerity and lack of inhibition.

Compare their encounter to the subplot that was being played out between Megan's mother and me as we watched and waited for our daughters.

While Kathleen and Megan greeted each other, I looked at Megan's mother and smiled. She gave me a slight grimace of recognition (we had seen each other coming and going at the day care center), then she quickly turned her attention back to the girls.

Kathleen and Megan talked about seeing each other in the movie theatre. I told Megan's mother that I thought it was a good movie. She was cordial. "The kids seemed to like it," she said.

Kathleen and Megan told each other that they are best friends.

"Isn't that cute," I said. Megan's mother responded by asking where Kathleen's mother was—in a tone that suggested I left my wife at home and brought my daughter to see "101 Dalmatians" as part of some sinister plot to seduce Mrs. Megan.

Kathleen and Megan hugged. I watched them and got a warm feeling. I looked up at Megan's mother. She had a look on her face that said, "Don't even think about it, buster." At the same time, she was fumbling around in her purse, presumably for her car keys, but it occurred to me that she may also have been going for the mace—just in case.

Of course, Mrs. Megan need not have been concerned. As a fellow 20th century adult, I was every bit as inhibited as she was.

But our children have no problems socializing. My daughter not only tells Megan that they are best friends, she tells my wife and me that we are her best friends as well. It has not yet occurred to her that by definition, a person can have only one "best" friend. And who am I to straighten her out on the subject? In fact, listening to Kathleen and Megan has caused me to re-examine the logic behind having one "best" friend.

Apparently, it's a rather arbitrary thing governed by semantics and the limitations of our language. Theoretically, we can have any number of "good" friends, perhaps another select group who could be called our "better" friends, and ultimately, one person who is our "best" friend. And while the "good-better-best" method may have worked fine as a marketing tool for Sears & Roebuck, it definitely has its limitations when applied to friendship. As near as I can tell, there is nothing, bar proper grammar, to prevent a person from having more than one "best" friend, and I would submit that proper grammar is insufficient grounds for forcing my daughter to choose between Daddy, Mommy or Megan as her "best" friend.

I'm sure that Mrs. Megan and I and most other adults had more than one best friend at some point early in our lives. Somewhere along the way, our inhibitions took over, but it doesn't have to stay that way. I suspect that one of the reasons we have children on this planet is to show adults the way back to expressing our emotions.

It's worked on this adult. After being told by my daughter that I am her best friend, and after returning the compliment a number of times, I have found those words easier to say. Also, by witnessing her liberal use of the phrase—to me, Mommy, Megan, Grandma, Grandpa, her teachers, and, of course, her best friends—I have realized that I am also empowered to tell as many people as I like that they are my best friends. And I have especially realized that I should say those words to my best friends.

I recently did just that. I told John, my best friend out in Idaho, that he is, in fact, my best friend. I always knew that, and I assumed he did. But when he later told me how much it meant to him that I would tell him such a thing, I realized that we should not take such knowledge for granted.

I've also learned that in most cases, if you want a hug, all you've got to do is ask for it. Unless, of course, you are talking to Mrs. Megan. This, I chose to try out with my wife. And to my great delight and pleasure, I got exactly what I asked for: a hug. No strings attached. What a deal.

So if you'd like to have some fun, let your kids show you the way. Call your best friend and say, "You're my best friend." If it feels good—and I think it will—call another best friend and repeat the process.

And when you run out of best friends to call, ask your spouse or your parent or your kid for a hug. If at first they go for the mace, be patient. Old habits are hard to break. But somewhere inside each of us, you can be sure there's a kid who wouldn't mind a hug.

A Note From My Sister

I want to tell you about something very personal. It's about a note I got from my youngest sister one Christmas. It made me very happy when I received it, but it also made me cry. So I debated for a long time whether I should show it to anybody. And finally, for a number reasons, I decided that I should tell other people about it.

I'll show you the note in a minute, but first, I have to tell you a few things about me and my sister and our family.

Our parents got divorced when I was ten. My youngest sister, Sharon, would have been two. Sharon and I, along with the rest of our brothers and sisters, stayed with our mother. Our father moved to another part of Louisville for a while, remarried, and eventually moved away to Massachusetts.

After a few of years of trying, Mom finally acknowledged that she could not raise seven kids on her own. My brothers and sisters—including Sharon—were put in an orphanage. By that time, I was fourteen and I had a part time job, so Mom kept me home with her.

Now before you go feeling sorry for me and saying, "What a noble little boy, taking a job at fourteen to help his mother pay the bills," you need to know that I was not helping with the bills—although I did buy some of my own clothes. But overall, I didn't make that much money. And what I did make, I spent on myself.

So I wasn't at home to help pay the bills. When you get right down to it, I think Mom kept me at home so she wouldn't be lonely.

Unfortunately, I was not the greatest of companions. In fact, I was nothing but trouble. I skipped school, snuck out late at night with my friends, went to beer parties and generally got into a lot of trouble. The culminating event came shortly before my fifteenth birthday when I skipped school one day, stole the keys to Mom's car, took some friends for a joy ride, and ended up wrecking the car.

After that, there were lots of talks about what to do with me. My Mom talked to me. My uncle talked to me. Our priest talked to me. And, of course, my probation officer talked to me. (I got a probation officer after I got caught shoplifting earlier that same year.) Everybody finally decided that the best thing to do was to have me go live with my father in the hope that he would provide more discipline.

The result for Sharon and me, though, was that due to the difference in our ages, our parents' divorce, and my juvenile delinquency, we never had a chance to get to know each other very well.

That bothered me a lot when I was growing up. Especially after I moved away and began to realize how important family is. And I felt guilty because my brothers and sisters spent several years in an orphanage, and I did not have to. And because I had abused that privilege so much that I further broke up our already broken home.

I went back to Louisville about once a year to visit while I was living with my father, and I went back more often after I was out on my own. But I was always very self-conscious when I went back. I had much in common with the divorced father who comes back and tries to force everything into what has commonly come to be known as "quality time." But unlike the tentative, divorced father, I did not have to deal with children who withheld their affection because they resented me leaving them. To my knowledge, my brothers and sisters never blamed me for anything that had happened in our family. Quite the contrary. They always seemed glad to see me, and they never held back. Still, I always felt that I needed to make things up to them, so I was always trying, sometimes awkwardly, to do something special whenever I visited.

My brothers and sisters are all grown up now. Sharon is married and has her own life: husband, daughter, son, career, the works. A lot of years have gone by. And all those years, I never knew what my brothers and sisters thought, if anything, of me and my visits and my efforts to do something special when I visited. Until I got this note from my little sister one Christmas:

Dear Mike, I thought I'd share a special memory that I think about every year about this time. It was a long time ago...I don't know how many years. It was one of the times you came down for Christmas. It was Christmas Eve as I remember, and we didn't have a tree yet, and when you came in, we went and got one. It was the first time I ever got to help pick out a tree. I don't remember if anyone else was with us or not. I just remember you and the tree. So every year when we're going to get a tree, I get a special feeling and remember you on that Christmas Eve and that tree and I smile. Thanks. Love, Sharon

That's the note, and there's not much else I want to say about it. Except that if there's anybody out there in the world that you like and feel good about—and if there is any reason at all to suspect that they may not know how you feel—for God's sake, tell them. I guarantee they'll appreciate it.

The EcoSphere

Hold the world in your hands. That's what the advertisement for EcoSphere says.

EcoSphere is a little glass ball. It really does fit in your hands. Inside the ball are several things: water, algae, bacteria and some tiny shrimp. It is billed as "man's first successful attempt to create a self-sustaining life system."

It's actually a pretty interesting idea. Sunlight provides energy for the algae and bacteria. They, in turn, supply food and oxygen for the shrimp. The shrimp contribute by producing carbon dioxide and "wastes," which keep the algae and bacteria alive. (Funny how the highest life form in most ecosystems ends up listing "wastes" among its major contributions.)

Developing this little self-sustaining world was no easy task, I'm sure. Yet I find something kind of unsettling about the whole thing. Maybe it's the fact that this little world was developed by scientists at

NASA's Jet Propulsion Lab. You'd think that our top rocket scientists would have more important things to do.

But on second thought, I can see where the delicate balance between creatures of the world would be of concern to any serious scientist.

So it must be something else about the EcoSphere that bothers me. It could be that this little item is being sold in catalogues as a Christmas gift idea. A very expensive gift idea at that. It goes for up to $500. You can buy one, set it on your desk or your bookshelf, study it, observe it, maybe meditate on it. The manufacturer boasts that the shrimp can live for more than five years.

They even got Carl Sagan to hype the EcoSphere when it first came out. Quoth Sagan regarding the organisms in the globe: "You find yourself worrying about them, rooting for them."

The commercialization bothers me a little. So does the notion of "owning" a little world. We can't really "own" life. The idea of holding it in the palm of your hand is a bit too much. It deifies man in an age when we would be better served by humility.

I also find it a little unsettling that you could find yourself pulling for or even identifying with a shrimp. That scares me. The creatures in the EcoSphere only live for five years or so. That's a pittance in the whole scheme of things. Then again, in the whole scheme of things, 70 or 80 years is also a pittance. Suddenly, the shrimp and I have more in common that I care to acknowledge. I'm not trapped inside a glass ball, but I'm not likely to leave the planet any time soon either.

But the more I think about it, the more I realize that the EcoSphere itself doesn't bother me. It might actually be a good thing for everybody to have one of these little items. Looking at the

EcoSphere from your desk chair is a little like looking at the Earth from the Moon. You feel kind of sorry for those little waste-producing shrimp. They are not long for this world. So an EcoSphere could serve as a constant reminder of our mortality and of the delicate balance amongst living creatures. It might raise our consciousness a little.

And in the end, that's what I find most troubling—not the EcoSphere, but the realization that our consciousness still needs raising. Too many people still disregard the concept of our own ecosystem. And because we haven't acknowledged the fact that we are all part of a very fragile ecosystem, we fail to treat the environment, the other creatures in the world—even other human beings—with proper respect and concern.

I probably will never own an EcoSphere. The idea of owning a world still bothers me. But I'm glad somebody invented it. It makes you think. And while it's not very pleasant to identify with a shrimp, it's probably a pretty important thing to do from time to time.

Little Arms Around My Neck

For Kathleen

After a marathon day of opening presents and nonstop play, you have collapsed exhausted on the living room floor. It is now my job to get you up and put you to bed. Christmas is over.

I try to wake you up, but you can barely open your eyes. "Carry me, Daddy," you say, and as I pick you up, you put your little arms around my neck.

You are almost three, and it occurs to me that there will not always be little arms around my neck. So I am taking nothing for granted. There is not a single little hug that doesn't go straight to my heart and give me a thousand reasons for being.

Sometimes in the middle of a hug, you threaten to "eat me up"—which consists of a tight hug accompanied by some loud chomping noises. When the chomping noises begin, it makes me think of

Maurice Sendak's *Where the Wild Things Are*, one of your favorite stories. It contains one of the best lines in all of literature.

Early in the story, a little boy named Max tells his mother he's going to eat her up, and she sends him to his room for being such a wild thing. Then Max imagines a land where he becomes king of all the wild things. The other wild things love Max and don't ever want him to leave. "Oh, please don't go," they say. "We'll eat you up, we love you so."

That's what comes to mind when I feel little arms around my neck and hear little chomping noises. So I never take hugs for granted.

And later, when you are older, when I am no longer able to lift you up and feel your little arms around my neck, I will not be sad. Instead, I will look forward to each new hug from you, allow myself to feel it and enjoy it and love it every bit as much as I felt and enjoyed and loved your hugs when you were a little girl.

And above all, I will hug you back.

Holiday Parties

No matter how many company holiday parties I go to, I never feel completely at ease. Fact is, you're essentially being asked to socialize with people you normally try to avoid.

Also, I have to confess to what may be inappropriate thoughts. For example, I begin to fantasize that our new intern might not mind if I were to catch her under the mistletoe. Or I imagine that this would be the perfect time to tell the president about my ideas for restructuring the company—which naturally include a promotion for me.

Of course, I know in my heart such actions would be inappropriate. But at the time, when one is caught up in the spirit of the holidays, such things seem not only appropriate, but logical. It's as if smooching with interns and schmoozing with the president are things I should have been doing all along.

Fortunately, not all my thoughts are so deplorable. I also find myself complimenting some of the people I genuinely enjoy working with.

There's something about the holiday season that forces you to search your soul for nice things to say—especially if someone catches you off guard and says something nice to you first. Unfortunately, I don't always have something nice to say about some of the people I work with. Which makes me really appreciate the people I can say something nice about.

All too often, I receive a compliment and find myself responding with something innocuous like, "Thank you, Earl. I enjoyed working with you on that direct mail piece, also." And while I suppose that's better than nothing, I enjoy it much more when I can say sincerely, "You're a good person, Fred. I'm glad we work together."

Of course, I then find myself wondering why I never complimented that particular person during the course of the year.

So in order to safeguard against career-ending miscues at the holiday party—and at the same time, to help encourage appropriate behavior throughout the rest of the year—I have two suggestions. Use these to guide your actions during the holiday season and throughout the year:

1. If it seems inappropriate in July, it's probably still inappropriate in December. White beards and Santa suits notwithstanding, you should keep your hands out of your coworker's stockings.

2. If it seems appropriate during the holidays, you should probably try doing it throughout the rest of the year. I appreciate it when someone tells me at the holiday party that they like working with me. But my best friends are the ones who have a kind word to say in the dog days of July or August.

Follow these two rules of thumb, and you'll come to be known as a decent and much valued coworker. You'll also get invited to a lot more holiday parties.

The Difference Between Men and Women

My sister called me for advice. She said "hello" to a guy at work, and now he keeps pestering her for a date. "I was just being friendly," she said.

"That's the difference between men and women," I told her. "Women are friendly; men are obsessed."

I hate to sound so cynical, but it's true. Many otherwise intelligent and worldly women don't seem to understand that if you make eye contact with a guy, he thinks you want to sleep with him. If you smile at him, he thinks you really want to sleep with him. And if you actually talk to him or laugh at one of his jokes...you don't want to know what he's thinking.

It might sound like you're just telling him that you want to use the copier. Or that he has mustard on his chin. Or maybe you're just a nice person who believes in saying "hello" to people when you see them. It doesn't matter. No matter how innocent your comment might seem to you, the guy will automatically analyze the encounter in terms of where you stand on the scale of desire to sleep with him.

Unfortunately, none of us are above this sort of thinking. I pride myself on being aware of this difference between men and women, yet when a coworker smiled at me recently, I sensed her desire and made a mental note to stay away from her in the future. I don't need that kind of trouble.

None of this is meant to imply that men should change. That's a moot point anyway. We fear change and are, for the most part, incapable of it. Nor should women change. But the next time you see a guy, you might want to start off with this disclaimer: "In no way does what I'm about to say imply that I have any desire whatsoever to sleep with you. I'm just being friendly." After that, it should be safe to go ahead and say "hello." He may still think you want to sleep with him, but he'll be so confused that you might actually be able to have a normal conversation while you're waiting to use the copier.

New Year's Resolutions

I don't make resolutions on New Year's Eve anymore.

Now before you categorize me as a New Year's "Scrooge," allow me to add that it's not because I think resolutions are a bad thing. For the most part, I think they may be a good thing. They give people goals, and goals help us live our lives in an orderly fashion.

But we also need hope, and my concern is that too many goals—especially goals in the form of New Year's resolutions—can have a bad affect on hope.

All too often, we rush blindly from one goal to another or from one project to another without really examining what we're doing. I've been guilty of this on more than one occasion. I love to take on household projects—paint the living room, build some new shelves in the basement, refinish that old table—all of which give me some degree of pleasure and satisfaction, but all of which, if taken on in quick succession, ultimately serve as distractions and diversions from our real purpose here.

What is our real purpose here? I won't pretend to be able to answer that question. Our purpose—and whatever meaning there is to our lives—is something we have to discover for ourselves. Some think meaning comes through the pursuit of knowledge. Others feel art and self expression hold the meaning of life. Still others feel that to leave behind a healthy, well-adjusted child is no small feat.

Whatever the meaning of life may be, I'm pretty sure it doesn't have to do with a fresh coat of paint on the living room wall. Not that there's anything wrong with doing a little home improvement—I personally find it relaxing at times—but we have to guard against letting such projects take on lives of their own.

So I don't make resolutions any more. I have enough things I'm trying to do in my life without putting more pressure on myself. Instead, what I do is to sit down sometime before the end of the year—and ideally, a few times during the year, too—and think about why I'm here and what I'm doing with my life. I figure that if I keep working on home improvements, I'm eventually going to have a pretty nice house. When that time comes, I want to make sure there's a pretty nice human being to occupy that house.

The Rose Parade

My father has lived in southern California for many years. He tells me the best time to be in southern California is on New Year's Day. And the best place to be is in Pasadena watching the Rose Parade.

There may be something to what he says. Some demographers have theorized that the Rose Parade may single-handedly be responsible for an influx on the order of 100,000 people into southern California every year. It seems that a lot of people all over the country watch the Rose Parade (and later in the day, the Rose Bowl football game) on television, and that gives them the final impetus to say, "The hell with the cold and the snow and the wind; California here I come." This seems to happen especially with fans of Big Ten teams—people who just happen to be watching the Rose Parade from the frigid environs of places like Michigan, Iowa, Ohio, Illinois and Wisconsin.

I've watched the Rose Parade on television, but I've never seen it in person. I doubt if I'll ever bother. However, on more than one occasion, I've looked at apartments along the parade route on Orange Grove Boulevard in Pasadena. That's an experience.

If you've watched the Rose Parade on television, you may not have an appreciation for what a grand thoroughfare Orange Grove Boulevard is. Orange Grove Boulevard is a wide street lined on both sides with palm trees. It's also lined with some multi-million dollar homes and some pretty nice luxury apartments—many of which provide spectacular views of the sun setting over downtown Los Angeles.

I first looked at an apartment on Orange Grove Boulevard (and first learned that I would never be able to afford such an apartment) in 1980. I had just graduated from college, and I had come to Los Angeles to look for a job. I sent out dozens of resumes but received only a handful of interviews—and no job offers. It was very frustrating. It was only later that I learned that, as a recent graduate with only a bachelors degree in business administration, I had no business applying for jobs like Vice President of Finance, Treasurer or Controller.

What I did have was lots of time to kill. So one day, while driving from downtown Los Angeles back to my father's house, I saw a sign saying "apartment for rent" on Orange Grove Boulevard. I decided to stop and look.

The apartment was open so I went in and looked around. To put it bluntly, it was the most spectacular apartment I had ever seen. The rooms were huge. And there was one long wall—it had to be 40 feet long—with a full-length picture window facing west, overlooking a pool, and beyond that, downtown Los Angeles and the Hollywood hills.

There were also some guys there doing some painting. I asked them about the rent. They told me it was $700 a month.

That may not seem terribly outrageous now. But this was 1980. What were you paying for rent back then? I was paying $175 a month for an apartment in Illinois. And that included all my utilities!

I eventually gave up on finding a job in Los Angeles and went back to Illinois where I finally found my first job. But as fate would have it, I ended up with a job in Los Angeles in 1987. I moved out there with my wife, who was pregnant at the time, and we settled into a little apartment east of Pasadena.

We were not particularly pleased with our accommodations, but it was all we could afford at the time. We stuck it out for a year there, my wife had our daughter, and we came to a crucial moment in our lives when we had to decide whether we would stay in southern California or move back to the Midwest.

This was not a simple process. And not one that could be resolved by taking in the Rose Parade. We mulled this decision over for several weeks.

During that time, we decided to look at other accommodations. If we stayed in southern California, we were not going to stay in our apartment. We quickly realized that it would be years before we could afford a house in the Los Angeles area (a two bedroom fixer-upper with a small lot was going for about ten times my salary at the time), so we started looking at other apartments.

And lo and behold, I found myself on Orange Grove Boulevard again. It also just so happened that the same apartment I had looked at in 1980 was again vacant. I couldn't resist looking at it—this time with my wife and infant daughter in tow. It was still spectacular. It had also gone up in price—to $1,700 per month.

We moseyed on down the street to another apartment building, still on Orange Grove Boulevard, but slightly more modest for the vicinity. The second apartment we looked at was also very large and well appointed. It lacked the spectacular view, but it was also $600 less per month. My wife and I liked it so much, we started talking about what we would have to do to be able to afford an $1,100 per month rent payment. We realized we could pull it off, but that it would take a lot of sacrifice and hard work. We'd have to take the money we were putting into savings and put it toward rent. My wife would have to go to work sooner than she planned, which meant finding day care for our daughter. In the meantime, I could do some freelance work evenings and weekends.

But somewhere along the way, sanity prevailed. We realized that we wanted more than a better apartment. We wanted a better life.

And that's the problem with looking at big, expensive apartments on streets like Orange Grove Boulevard. Things like that throw us off track. You look at a big, new house, or a luxury apartment, or a new car, or a big screen television, and you realize that all those things could be yours with more money. So you immediately start looking for ways to get more money.

And while there's nothing inherently wrong with having money to provide for your family or to do things you enjoy, none of those things in themselves are the answer. A bigger apartment isn't going to make you happy. And once you've covered you basic needs, more money isn't necessarily going to make you happy either.

Fortunately, my wife and I realized all of that before we got in too deep. (Actually, there was not moment of epiphany. It was more instinctual than anything.) We moved back to the Midwest where we could live comfortably within our means, and where we worked at strengthening our marriage and raising a family. Not that those things can't be done in southern California. But I would argue that there are so many competing priorities that maintaining a marriage and healthy family is definitely more difficult there.

I've still never been to the Rose Parade in person. And I don't usually watch it on television either. But once in a while, I'll catch a glimpse of it on New Year's morning, and I'm reminded of the spectacular apartment and the prestigious address that could have been mine. But at the same time, I realize that I don't want the fancy apartment anymore. I never really did. All I really wanted was a good place to raise my daughter. And more important, I wanted to be able to spend time with her. And here in the cold, snowy environs of Illinois in January, I have all the time in the world.

10

The Top Ten

At the end of each year, everybody scrambles to come up with the "Top Ten." The top ten songs. Top ten movies. Top ten news stories. On New Year's Eve 1999, somebody even came up with a list of the top ten historical events of the 20th Century. Pretty heady stuff.

I would like to propose a more modest list. A personal top ten. What would you list among your own top ten accomplishments last year? What were the ten nicest things that happened to you? What were the ten strangest things? What were your ten best days?

The first time I tried to come up with a personal top ten list, I had trouble thinking up ten of anything. It seemed not much had happened in my life. And of course, despite the fact that not much had happened, it also seemed that I had been busier than heck.

I was tempted at that point to make a "to do" list, but we always end up carrying those around like so much excess baggage. Instead, I just made a list of ten things that were going on in my life at the time. Sort of a personal balance sheet to describe where I was and what I was doing.

Back then, I was trying to finish work on a degree. I had some debts to pay off. I wasn't getting along very well with my boss. I wasn't getting along very well with my wife. I had a number of household projects that I had been putting off. I wrote it all down, then folded the list up and tucked it in my wallet.

When I pulled out my list a year later, I was amazed how much things had changed in my life. Some of my problems were gone. Some new problems had taken their place. But overall, I had accomplished much more than I would have imagined.

Since then, I produce a balance sheet and a list of accomplishments every year. Some of the things that made my list this year: I did more writing last year. I also argued less with my wife. (I'm sure the two are related.) I paid off some debts, saved some money, started one new friendship and renewed an old one. I even started piano lessons again—something I had started and stopped years ago.

Among my ten best days, I'd count any of the dozen or so that I took my daughter to the playground so she could play, after which we sat and watched the evening sky turn orange, red, pink and purple.

In the strange category, I was asked to join a group of local citizens who are campaigning against substance abuse. That's strange because when I was younger, I probably could have served as their poster boy. So I had ambiguous feelings about joining this group. But in the end, I realized they were primarily against "abuse" (as opposed to "substance"), so I joined their cause.

The result of all this is that I highly recommend taking a look at where you've been and what's going on around you right now. And if you need a confidence builder, make a "done" list instead of a "to do" list. List ten things that you've done in the past year, then check them off.

You'll find that you're not drifting aimlessly through life. Whether it was conscious or not, you've set a course for yourself. The things that are important to you will become obvious because they will crop up again and again on your list of accomplishments. Or else you'll notice that after listing your accomplishments, you still have an empty feeling. Some one particular thing isn't on the list. In either case, you'll learn what's important to you, and you can determine whether you are on course, slightly off course, or in need of a refresher course in cartography.

In our trek through life, we tend to revisit the same places. Sometimes the best way to figure out where you're going is to look at where you've already been.

The Scrabble Tournament

It was January 1998 and I found myself a passenger in a car hurtling across a wintry Midwestern landscape en route to downtown Chicago where I had an appointment with destiny. Yes, my coworkers from the Northern Illinois Gas corporate communications department and I were on our way to play in the big charity fundraiser Scrabble tournament in the hoity-toity digs of the Chicago Athletic Club on Michigan Avenue. Little did I know that before the night was over, I would test my mettle in a head-to-head competition against the reigning National Scrabble Champion. But I'm getting ahead of myself...

I'm not exactly sure how I got into this thing. I am not a big Scrabble player. I had played enough, I suppose, mostly when on vacation visiting my friends, John and Julie, out in Idaho, where Scrabble made for a fun and relaxing after-dinner activity. John is a published author and professor of creative writing and Julie is a freelance writer/editor, so they were excellent opponents. Beyond that, I played a few friendly games now and then, but I had never been in a tournament. Not even close. But this was a charity fundraiser for the Chicago Lighthouse for the Blind, and my boss got the company to sponsor a team, so there I was.

When we entered the Chicago Athletic Club, it was everything you would expect of an exclusive and historic downtown men's athletic club. Doormen greeted us and held open the lead-glass doors. The lobby consisted of marble floors, heavy dark paneling, a 30-foot-high ornamental ceiling, sparkling chandeliers and hushed tones. We were led to a bank of elevators and then taken up to the fourth floor, which was decorated like the interior of a British country manor: timbered ceilings, oriental rugs, fireplaces wide enough to hang a hammock, overstuffed chairs in comfortably worn leather, and settees covered in elegant but manly silk fabric of deep maroon and dark green reminiscent of a jungle somewhere in the far reaches of the British Empire. I ordered a Beefeater and tonic and mingled while participants registered for the tournament.

I was chatting up the team from the Tribune Company when there was a major hubbub at the entrance. I made my way over and realized what was going on: the event's guest of honor, the National Scrabble Champion, had arrived. He was an unimposing fellow... early 30s, about 5'8", modest smile, neatly trimmed black hair that went a little too far down the back of his neck…but he was quickly surrounded by a bevy of blushing Scrabble beauties. Yes, it was mostly low heels and there may have been a little too much polyester involved—and I'm almost positive they all wore corrective lenses—

but there was no mistaking the pheromones in the air. The Scrabble Champ was in the house, and it was every articulate woman for herself.

Once the hubbub of the Champ's grand entrance subsided, the tournament organizers got on the public address system to officially welcome everyone, go over a few ground rules and get the tournament started. We were playing in teams of three, and we would work our way up the ladder in a single-elimination tournament until we had a winner.

My teammates and I had an easy time of it against our first opponents—an overmatched trio of young copywriters from the Leo Burnett Agency. That will teach them to send children to do a senior account manager's job. But I was worried when I was informed of our next opponent: the editors of Playboy magazine.

Think what you will of Playboy, but the fact is their magazine had a reputation for publishing high-quality fiction and nonfiction. Now we were about to sit down across a Scrabble board from their jet-setting editors. I wasn't sure what to expect, but I was pretty sure it would be either a trio of bunnies in horn-rimmed glasses or Hugh Hefner himself with two of his girlfriends in "X" and "O" t-shirts. In any case, it was going to take all of our powers of concentration to focus on the game. We steeled ourselves and went to face our opponents...and soon found ourselves sitting opposite three of the nerdiest twenty-somethings you ever saw.

"You're the editors of Playboy?" I asked.

"Well, not *the* editors," said the lone female editor.

"But we do a lot of the editing," said one of the guys.

"Yeah, a lot," said the other guy.

"Okay," I said. "Let's play."

They were tough opponents, and they quickly had us on the ropes. And the further into the game we got, I noticed my teammates were relying more and more on me to come up with words.

Midway through the game, our opponents put down WRINKLE and picked up 50 bonus points for using all of their letters. They high-fived each other, adjusted their glasses and sat back to watch us squirm. We were down by 45 points and looking at this rack: AEORRSV.

"There's got to be something we can do with this," I said. If nothing else, we could put an S on WRINKLE and make WRINKLES. I started moving the tiles around...VARROES...VAROSER...REVAROS...

Eventually, I came to RESAVOR and SAVORER.

"Those aren't real words, are they?" said one of my teammates.

"I'm not 100 percent sure, but I think they are," I said.

We debated for a few moments which one to play. In the end, I was slightly more comfortable with SAVORER. I explained to my teammates, "You can put an 'ER' on almost any verb and define it as 'One who does whatever.'" So we played SAVORER.

The Playboy editors examined the word. "Savorer," said one of them. "One who savors. Nice play." We got points for SAVORER, points for WRINKLES, plus 50 points for using all of our letters. We never looked back after that, and soon we were saying good-bye to the editors of Playboy magazine and moving on to the next round.

There was a bit of intermission first though, so we took a break and had another round of cocktails. I was standing next to one of the big open-hearth fireplaces at the Chicago Athletic Club, swirling my Beefeater and tonic, recounting the SAVORER/RESAVOR dilemma and our ultimate victory to anyone who would listen when we heard this announcement: "The National Scrabble Champion has graciously agreed to an exhibition to raise additional funds for the Chicago Lighthouse," said the announcer. "The Champion will take on any and all comers in a mini-game of Scrabble for a donation of twenty dollars per entrant." I don't know if it was the endorphins from my recent victory or the gin, but the announcer had no sooner put down the microphone than I blurted out, "I'll play him!"

The circle of people around me applauded, and I was simultaneously congratulated and ushered across the room to the registration table. While one of the organizers put my name at the top of the list of challengers, I looked over at the Champ. He was standing off to the side of the registration table. In his hand was a cola of some sort. On his face was a smug smile. And by his side were a half dozen of the best-spelling women in Illinois. I suddenly felt very overmatched. The organizer took my twenty dollars.

"Where do I go now?" I asked.

"Let me sign up the others, then we'll get started," she said.

I looked behind me. There were a dozen other people waiting to sign up for the challenge.

"Looks like you have time to 'resavor' the moment," said the Champ. His entourage of spelling-bee queens buzzed with laughter.

I searched my brain for a witty retort. "Yeah," I said. And then I retreated to the men's room to gather my wits.

Walking into the men's room at the Chicago Athletic Club is like walking back in time. You can pull a comb out of a jar of blue disinfectant and comb your hair. You can refresh yourself with a splash of Pinaud Clubman After Shave Lotion or Clubman Citrus Musk Eau de Cologne. And best of all, you can pee into a urinal full of crushed ice.

I don't know whose job it was to keep the urinals full of crushed ice, but if he had been present, I would have thanked him. There's just something about melting some ice that restores a man's confidence. I finished up, washed my hands, splashed on some cologne and braced myself to face the National Scrabble Champion.

I walked back out into the faux English country manor that was the fourth floor of the Chicago Athletic Club and heard my name on the public address system: "Mike O'Mary…report to the registration table for the Champion Challenge!" It was time.

I strolled confidently to the table. The National Scrabble Champion was standing next to the event organizers.

"I'm Mike O'Mary," I said to one of the organizers. She introduced me to the Champion. We shook hands.

"Thank you for supporting this event," he said.

I wouldn't be thrown off by niceties. "Let's play," I said.

There were about 100 people at the tournament that night, and every single one of them gathered around as the organizers led the Champ and me to a table that had been set up for the Champion Challenge. The Champ and I sat face-to-face across the small square table. One of the organizers explained the rules: the Champ and I would each get the same seven letters. We would have 60 seconds to come up with our best word. Whoever came up with the word worth the most points would be declared the winner.

While the organizer was explaining the rules, the crowd gathered tight around our little table. Some of them pressed in a little too close.

"Mmmm...someone smells good," said a female voice behind me. I looked over my shoulder. It was an attractive black woman.

"Clubman Citrus Musk," I said. She smiled at me. Her date, a very suave looking Billy Dee Williams type, smiled too and gave me a thumbs up.

"Could we have a little breathing room?" said the Champ. His tone conveyed that this was more than a request. Volunteers stepped in to push the crowd back. We were ready to begin.

An organizer stepped up to the table and placed seven tiles face down in front of the Champ and me. I looked up at the Champ. He looked as cool and calm as ever...imagine James Bond at a Monte Carlo baccarat table, sipping a very dry martini—except he has a little too much bristly hair going down the back of his neck and his martini is a Mr. Pibb.

"Are you ready?" asked the organizer.

"Ready," said the Champ.

"Ready," said I.

"Begin!" said the organizer.

The Champ and I picked up our tiles, placed them on our racks and studied them. Neither of us moved any tiles around at first, and it occurred to me that perhaps the Champ didn't need to rearrange tiles. Perhaps he could just see things in his head. Maybe that's why he was the Champ. Or maybe he was just messing with my head. Maybe he was trying to intimidate me by not touching his tiles, which would make me feel self-conscious about the idea of touching my tiles, which meant I wouldn't be able to rearrange my tiles, which would put me at a disadvantage since I normally like to move my tiles around.

"Fifty seconds," said the organizer.

Damn! I thought to myself. I just wasted 10 seconds trying to out-think the Champ. He was good, no doubt about it. Without even trying, he had gotten into my head and thrown me off my game. But I wasn't going to let myself get caught up in his head games…not in a 60-second dash to Scrabble immortality. I decided right then and there that win or lose, I was going to play my way.

"Forty seconds," said the organizer. I started rearranging my tiles.

The Champ and I were each dealt the following letters: EFIOMT. Yes, I know…that's only six letters. There was a seventh letter, but I can't remember what it was. It doesn't matter anyway. Neither the Champ nor I were able to use that seventh letter, so I can pretty much guarantee that it was unusable. The Champ and I each played our hand using those six letters: EFIOMT.

I was rearranging my letters and coming up with some different options…FIT…MET…OFT…but nothing good. Meanwhile, the Champ still hadn't lifted a finger. He just sat there studying his tiles, still trying to get into my head. But I was playing my own game… staying within myself. I kept rearranging my tiles: TOME…TIME… EMIT…MITE…OMIT…

"Thirty seconds."

Finally, the Champ started rearranging his tiles. And oddly enough, the fact that he was following my lead bolstered my confidence.

But that little boost in confidence was accompanied by a shot of adrenalin, which in turn made it more difficult to concentrate, and suddenly, I couldn't think straight. I was losing it. I continued to rearrange my letters, but it was all nonsense: MIFO…FIMO…TIMO…TEFI…FIOT…nothing!

"Twenty seconds!"

I realized this was probably just as the Champ had planned. He was playing it cool, and I had played right into his hands. But I refused to give up. Focus, I said to myself. Concentrate. That's when I heard the little voice in my head.

"See the word."

It started as a whisper, but it kept repeating and it grew louder and more drawn out with each repeat: "Seeeee the worrrrrd."

It kept running through my head over and over again—and then I realized the voice wasn't coming from inside my head…it was coming from somewhere behind me. I turned around and watched as Billy Dee Williams did a stage whisper: "Seeeeee the worrrrrrd."

It was meant to be supportive, and I realized then that he and most of the rest of the people in the room were all pulling for me to knock off this Scrabble gunslinger of a champion who had blown into town intent on showing off his erudite ways and wooing all of our intelligent women, only to blow out of town the next day, leaving in his wake a trail of scattered Scrabble tiles, disillusioned lady literati, and humiliated but fragrant men. So I should have been flattered. But instead, I found the whispering very distracting—and the clock was counting down.

"Ten seconds," said the organizer.

"Seeeeeee the worrrrrrrd," said Billy Dee.

"Everything all right over there?" asked the Champ.

"Could we have quiet, please?" I yelled.

The room fell dead silent. My powers of concentration came back in a rush, and I could see not only the word, but the theme of my entire life. The structure, the design, the grand pattern…it was all perfectly clear now.

"Time," said the organizer. "Put down your words."

"After you," said the Champ.

I smiled, calmly selected my tiles one-by-one, and laid down my word: MOTIF.

Billy Dee Williams and his date and the 98 other onlookers broke into a round of applause.

"Nicely done," said the Champ.

"Thank you," I said.

"Now for your word," said the organizer to the Champ.

The Champ didn't bother with putting down his tiles one-by-one. He picked them all up in one hand and laid them before us in an omnipotent motion, as if to say, "In the beginning was the Word, and the Word was…FOMITE."

FOMITE?

"What the hell is FOMITE?" I said, before I could stop myself.

There was a quiet gasp from the audience at my crude inquiry. The organizers and volunteers instinctively moved in, lest I pull a blade and try to cut the Champ.

"It's an inanimate object that serves to transmit infectious organisms," said the Champ.

"It's in the dictionary," said somebody in the audience, holding up a pocket electronic Scrabble Dictionary.

"FOMITE?" I said. But the world was already moving on.

"Good game," said the Champ. He stood and held out his hand to me. I stood up and shook his hand, then one of the organizers yelled, "Next!" and I was ushered away.

I won't bore you with details of the rest of the Scrabble tournament at the Chicago Athletic Club in 1998. Most of the details of the remainder of that evening are kind of fuzzy in my memory anyway. I know that we lost our third round game by a wide margin, and I recall that my coworkers observed a somber and respectful silence on the drive home later that night. But the thing that sticks with me most was my walk through the crowd after my loss to the Champ. The Tribune Company representatives gave me a pat on the back as I went by. The young copywriters from Leo Burnett shook my hand and said, "Better than we could have done." The editors of Playboy magazine were genuinely bummed: "We thought you had him with 'MOTIF,' man!" And one of my coworkers came over and put an arm around me and asked, "Are you all right?"

"I'm fine," I said. "I just need a minute." So they all went off a left me alone by the fireplace with my thoughts. I wasn't alone for long though. I soon sensed a presence behind me. I turned around and saw Billy Dee Williams and his girlfriend.

"FOMITE," said Billy Dee. He was shaking his head in a motion that conveyed both disbelief and sympathy.

"Yeah, FOMITE," I said.

Billy Dee shook his head again. "That's rough," he said.

"Yeah," said his girlfriend.

"What are you going to do now?" asked Billy Dee.

"Nothing," I said. "I'll just keep playing."

Billy Dee nodded. "That's right, man. Just keep playing." He gave me a fist bump.

"You, too," I said. "See the word."

Billy Dee nodded again. "That's right," he said. Then he turned to his girlfriend. "C'mon, Baby. We got a game to play."

They turned to walk away, but his girlfriend looked back over her shoulder and smiled at me. "Bye, honey," she said. Then she turned to Billy Dee Williams and whispered, "You should get you some of that Clubman stuff."

Billy Dee turned to his girlfriend. "How many letters in 'Clubman,' Baby?" he asked.

"Seven," she said.

"That's right, Baby," said Billy Dee. "Seven." He smiled at her and she smiled back, and as they walked back in to the Scrabble tournament, I saw the grand pattern of my life clearly again and saw that it was time to break out of that pattern and make a change for the better.

Dog Days

We are in the dog days of winter. I can tell by watching my dog.

Normally when I let my dog in the house, she stops just inside the door so I can wipe her feet. Last week, when it was bitterly cold outside, I opened the door and Kallie darted in, ran straight to the kitchen, grabbed my cheeseburger off my plate, and took off running.

In the past, Kallie has chewed up pillows, eyeglasses, computer diskettes and numerous other items—but it usually happens when she has been home alone all day. She doesn't normally act like that when I'm around.

I told a coworker about my stupid dog, and my coworker told me that her dog had been acting weird, too. One night, while she was watching the news, her dog started growling at Dan Rather. Then, when she tried to pull the dog away from the TV, the dog snapped at her.

My guess is that our dogs are suffering from cabin fever. And if our dogs are suffering, we probably are, too. Tempers are short, we are irritable and we do irrational things. Maybe we snap at people when we are normally patient and polite. Or we gnash our teeth and gnaw on our pillows when we hear politicians talk about the budget. And at some point every winter, we inevitably cross the line: we march into the living room while everybody else is watching TV, pick up the remote control and start flipping through channels like madmen.

Yes, things are getting bad. But don't worry. Spring is just around the corner—just another severe winter storm or two away. So until then, hang in there. And in the meantime, if you feel like grabbing somebody's cheeseburger, make sure you can outrun them.

Lucky Duck

The university in my hometown has a large pond on its grounds. Locally, it's referred to as "The Lagoon." As soon as the weather gets warm in the spring, hundreds of ducks fly in to make the pond their temporary home, and people from all over town bring their children to see the baby ducklings.

The ducks know a good thing when they see one, and they cruise the pond, accepting a slice of bread here, leftover French fries there. The only thing that spoils this otherwise serene setting is that some of the ducks fight with each other over food or chase kids around looking for a handout. Meanwhile, the smaller, more timid ducks hang back and go hungry. Some people throw breadcrumbs into the midst of the ducks and let nature take its course. Others seem to resent the aggressive ducks. They ignore them and throw crumbs to the timid ducks instead.

The best time at the lagoon comes earlier in the year, before the warm weather and ducks arrive. In winter, people go to the lagoon to ice skate. Even on a busy evening you can find a remote spot and skate in solitude. If you stop skating for a moment, you can hear the fragile sound of ice creaking beneath your feet. And if the night is clear, you can look up and see a sky full of stars creaking their way across the universe.

Best of all, there are no pesky ducks around.

I go to the lagoon in the winter when I want to be alone. On a clear winter night in a peaceful Midwestern town, it's a nice place to be.

* * *

I went to the lagoon on the night I heard about Joey Russo. The lagoon is a long way from Germantown, the blue-collar neighborhood of shotgun houses in Louisville where Joey and I grew up. In winter, kids were more likely to be dribbling a cold, gritty basketball in the alley behind Louie Eberhardt's house than they were to be ice-skating.

Joey Russo lived on the fringes of Germantown, in a little apartment above a bar at the corner of Burnett and Shelby Streets. Joey was the tough guy in our neighborhood. The local bully.

I first encountered Joey Russo at St. Elizabeth Elementary School. He was a year older than the rest of our class, having been held back to repeat the second grade. I got halfway through the school year without any trouble from him, then one day, a strange thing happened.

Our class was outside for recess after lunch. I was leaning against the short fence that separated the boy's side of the playground from the girl's side, and the next thing I knew, Kathy Johnson was standing a foot or so away from me on the other side of the fence. It was pretty unusual for a boy and a girl to be standing so close to each other at recess, but nobody seemed to notice. Then, suddenly, it happened: Kathy Johnson, very quietly, very calmly, very gently, leaned over and kissed me.

I had no idea how to act in that situation, so I did the only thing that made sense: I turned and ran as fast as I could in the opposite direction. Not that I minded being kissed by Kathy Johnson. On the contrary. She was one of the prettiest and smartest girls in school, and she was to be my girlfriend for the next two years. But I did mind being kissed in public. It felt to me that everybody was staring at me after the kiss, but in actuality, it was a nonevent. No one had noticed—no one except Joey Russo.

Joey cornered me a few days later while I was waiting to walk Kathy Johnson home after school.

"What are you doing here?" he asked.

"Nothing," I said.

Joey smiled. "You're waiting for Kathy Johnson, ain't ya?"

I hesitated for a moment, then answered, "Yes."

"You like her, don't you?" he asked.

"Yes."

"She likes you, too, don't she?" he asked.

"I guess," I said.

Joey walked around me, sizing me up.

"I like her, too," he said, "but I saw her kiss you the other day."

Upon hearing those words, I prepared myself for the worst: Joey Russo was going to kick my little seven-year-old butt.

"Don't worry. I ain't going to do nothing to you," he said. "If she likes you, that's all right." Then Joey started to walk away. Before he got very far, he turned and added, "Be nice to her."

His final words struck me as very odd. They came not so much as a threat or a warning (as in, "Be nice to her or I'll kick your butt"), but more as a piece of friendly advice—and more than that, as a piece of friendly advice that he knew he didn't really need to give.

I didn't have any more run-ins with Joey Russo for several years after that. During that time, he was in and out of trouble—if not for fighting, then for stealing, talking back to the teachers or skipping school.

Then, when I was 11 years old, I once again found myself face-to-face with Joey Russo. It was a hot, humid summer night. I was playing in the front yard when all of a sudden, there was a huge commotion from around the corner at the Gerard family's house. Somebody was yelling, and I heard a fence gate clang open and shut several times. I ran toward the noise and as I turned the corner, I ran right into Joey Russo.

There was a black kid with him, but the kid kept on running. Joey stopped though and looked right at me. He didn't say anything, but he walked slowly past—staring at me the whole time—then continued on down the middle of the street at a jog.

I watched him run off, then I went to the Gerards' house. It turned out that some bikes had been stolen. The Gerard kids were distraught, and Mr. Gerard was ready to kill someone. I walked up to him and said, "I know who did it."

It occurred to me later that I did not really know who did it. When I saw Joey Russo, he was on foot, which meant someone else must have stolen the bikes. But when the police arrived, I told them that I had seen Joey Russo running away.

The police knew who Joey was, and they took me with them to look for him. At one point, we turned the corner into Eberhardt's alley and spotted a kid on a bike. But before the police could close in, the kid cut through a backyard and disappeared. After that, the police gave up and took me home.

The whole thing left me with an uneasy feeling. Had I done the right thing in telling on Joey? Was it him we saw racing down the alley? I didn't hear any more about the stolen bikes until that fall.

* * *

Each Friday during the football season, one of the big high school games is played at Manual Stadium in Germantown. One particular night, I was hanging out with my friend, Mark Schmid, at his house across the street from the stadium. Mark's older brother, Matt, was also there with some of his friends.

Matt and the older guys called themselves "The Clique," and they were apparently expecting trouble that night. Kenny Vessels had been cornered and beaten up earlier that day by several black guys along a stretch of Shelby Street. One of the black guys, known only as Rodney, had threatened Kenny with a gun. Tonight, Kenny was prepared: he had his father's gun and he was showing it around.

While the older guys talked on the front porch, Mark was trying to get me to slap box with him. Slap boxing was like boxing except you were supposed to land your punches with an open hand—a slap.

Mark was pretty quick with his hands, so I tried to avoid slap boxing with him. Generally speaking, it was the exception rather than the rule when a slap box fight didn't turn into a regular fight. Mark ended up slap boxing with Vince Metz, one of the older guys.

The guys in The Clique were still talking about Rodney when Joey Russo came by. Joey knew Rodney. Shelby Street where Joey lived was more or less the boundary line between black and white neighborhoods. The guys seemed to be arguing about Rodney. After a few minutes, Joey walked over to where Mark and Vince were sparring.

"Let me take him on, Vince," said Joey.

"Sure." Vince walked away and Joey stepped in.

You could tell Mark did not really want to slap box Joey Russo, but Joey insisted. He taunted Mark into attacking, then ducked under Mark's punches, slapping Mark once on the way under the punch and again on the way back up. This went on over and over again until Matt Schmid quietly observed, "That's enough, Joey."

"No problem," said Joey. He let Mark walk away. Then he looked at me. "How about you?"

"No thanks," I tried. But everybody was watching, so I took my place for my slap box fight with Joey, thinking for the second time in my life, this is it: I'm gonna get my butt kicked by Joey Russo.

Our fight started with Joey dancing around, feinting punches while I concentrated on defense. All the while, he was taunting me to throw a punch, which I finally did. Not only did I fail to land my punch, I found myself getting slapped with a counter punch before my right arm was even fully extended. It wasn't much of a fight.

Gradually, the other guys lost interest, and our bout eased to the pace of a casual sparring match. Before I knew it, I found myself in a conversation with Joey Russo.

"You told on me about those bikes, didn't you?" Joey said.

"Yeah, I did," I said.

"That's what I figured," he said.

"What happened?" I asked.

"Nothing," said Joey. "The cops tried to blame me for it, but they never found the bikes, so there was nothing they could do."

I didn't say anything. After a moment, Joey dropped his arms and turned toward the bright lights of the stadium.

I dropped my arms, too, and watched him. He was only a year older than me, but he had the same worn, expressionless face as the old men that used to shuffle into the Blue Motor Coach bus station to get warm in winter. That could be Joey, too, I thought. Shuffling around downtown, looking for warmth, being chased off wherever he went.

I was feeling sorry for Joey, when suddenly, he turned and swung at me, stopping an inch from my face and smiling a nasty smile.

"You know something?" he said; "sometimes you ain't too smart."

At that moment, Kenny Vessels and the members of The Clique started down the driveway.

"You coming, Joey?" Kenny asked.

"Rodney's a lot of talk," said Joey. "Don't go looking for trouble."

"You coming or not?" responded Kenny.

And with that, Joey left me and Mark and went with the older guys.

* * *

There wasn't any trouble that night, but there were more and more clashes between black and white kids in Germantown as the year went on. That was 1967. It seemed like every time you looked at the television, Martin Luther King was leading a march somewhere. When he came to Louisville, my parents took me to my grandmother's house. We watched on television as Martin Luther King led a march through town.

"Somebody is going to kill that man," declared my grandmother. It was not a threat. It was not a wish. She was simply stating what she felt to be obvious.

When King was shot in 1968, there were fights all over town. It was nothing compared to the rioting that went on in other cities, but things had changed. Nobody dribbled basketballs in the alley behind the Eberhardts' house. It was a dangerous place. White kids stood at one end of the alley calling names and throwing rocks at black kids, who stood at the other end of the alley and did likewise. Our neighborhood—our world—was not as nice a place as it had once been. It was as if the fabric of the whole country had unraveled to the point where we were all living on the fringe. And I came to realize that for Joey Russo, who had spent his whole life on the fringe, the world had never been a nice place.

I did not see Joey for a long time after our slap box fight, but the memory of that night stuck with me. Once again, with an opportunity to hurt or humiliate me, Joey Russo had let me off the hook.

Not too long after that, I began to get into trouble myself. After the sixth grade, I left St. Elizabeth for Highland Junior High School. While at Highland, I got into progressively more trouble until by the ninth grade, I barely passed, getting six Ds and one F after skipping 40 some-odd days of school that year. My problems at school, combined with an arrest for shoplifting and my parents' divorce, meant I had enough troubles without worrying about Joey Russo any more. I ended up moving away to live with my father.

The next time I saw Joey Russo was a few years later when I was back to visit my mother for the holidays. I saw Mark Schmid and a lot of the other guys I had always hung around with, but I was surprised to find that Joey Russo was now hanging out in our part of Germantown. Joey had always hung out with the tough guys, the older guys, even some of the black guys. He didn't really fit in with my mischievous—but not necessarily tough—friends. Yet there he was, hanging around, trying to fit in.

One night, a bunch of us were in front of my mother's house with nothing to do when somebody suggested that we go ice-skating. Mark Schmid said he could get his parents' car, so the rest of us went to tell our parents what we were planning to do. Everybody went their separate ways except Joey, who just kind of hung around in front of my house.

Inside the house, my mother gave me five dollars—two for admission, three to spend—but rather than wait outside with Joey, I stayed in the house. I didn't go out until everybody else was back. Then as we were getting into Mark's car, Joey asked me if I would lend him the money to go ice-skating. This caught me off guard, but I knew right away that I did not want to lend him the money. I knew I would never get it back. I also knew that, although no one had said the words, none of us really wanted Joey to come with us.

"No," I said. "I only have enough for me." I said this knowing that I could have given him two dollars for admission and still have had enough left to pay for myself. I said this also knowing that Joey might simply decide to take my money.

We then waited for Joey to ask the other guys if any of them would lend him the money. But Joey didn't ask. He just waited to see if anybody else would speak up. No one did. After a moment, we piled into the car without Joey. As we pulled away, I saw him head back toward his house on Shelby Street, walking right down the middle of the street.

That was the last time I saw Joey Russo. He didn't come to our neighborhood any more. Over the years, I heard he was constantly in trouble until finally he ended up in prison. I never heard why, but I assumed it was for stealing. A few years later, I heard he was out and that he had a girlfriend over on Mulberry Street. People said he was trying to straighten out his life.

Then one day, his girlfriend's ex-boyfriend showed up on Mulberry Street and found Joey there and shot Joey in the chest. Joey died on his girlfriend's front porch, three blocks from where he grew up, two blocks from St. Elizabeth Elementary. He was 23 years old.

* * *

Sometimes we hear about somebody like Joey and we say, "Well, he was in and out of trouble...he had just gotten out of prison...he was always with the wrong crowd...what did you expect?" And we're right. All those things were true.

And yet, at the risk of sounding like his mother, I will say that Joey Russo was not a bad kid. He deserved better. He was no saint—

he sometimes pushed people around—but maybe that was the only way he knew. And seeing how reluctant some people (including me) were to do something for him when he asked, it's a wonder he wasn't meaner and nastier and more spiteful than he was.

In the end, living on the fringe must have worn on him. He wanted a nice girl like Kathy Johnson, or nice friends like some of the guys in my neighborhood, or just a nice place to visit like the ice rink or his girlfriend's house on Mulberry Street. He wanted out of the tough-guy/bully role, out of our dreary, blue-collar neighborhood.

But he didn't fit in, so when he came around, we told him, "No."

On the night I heard about Joey Russo's death, I went to the lagoon and skated. And now, when I'm out on clear, crisp nights, I look up at the loose fabric of our universe and think there must be some place in it for people like Joey Russo. Wherever it is, I hope Joey has found it and that it is a nice place.

Meanwhile, back here on the creaky ice of the lagoon, I realize how lucky I am to have a nice place to visit...a nice life to live. And while I have difficulty remembering much about the skating rink I visited 25 years ago, I have no trouble at all bringing Joey Russo to mind, recalling that he was, in fact, not a bad person, and wishing things had been better for him in his short life, wishing I had lent him a few dollars to go ice skating when I had the chance to do so, and thinking if I had the opportunity today, I would bring little Joey Russo to this frozen lagoon and ask him to skate with me.

And later this year, when the ice melts and the ducks come, I will feed them all.

Heaven

It was a spur-of-the-moment thing: "Put on your winter coat and get a warm blanket," I told my daughter. "We're going out to look at Christmas lights."

When I was a kid, one of the highlights of the holiday season was driving around town looking at everyone's Christmas decorations. Our family—seven kids and two adults—would pile into the station wagon and off we'd go.

Normally, my father and a car full of kids was a volatile mixture. But it was different at Christmas. When you put us in our pajamas, wrapped us in our blankets, and took us out for a late-night ride to look at Christmas decorations, it was actually peaceful in that station wagon.

But that was then. My days of riding around in pajamas and blankets are pretty much over. However, one of the privileges of being a parent is that your children provide you with a legitimate excuse to do some of the things you haven't done since you were a kid. And so, we set out in search of wonderful, awe-inspiring Christmas lights.

Unfortunately, things seldom go according to plan when we try to recreate our childhood. Some little variable always changes the equation, sometimes for the better, sometimes for worse. Such was the case that evening when I took Kathleen, my little six-year-old variable, out for a Christmas drive.

I had in mind a little subdivision in the neighboring town of Sycamore, Illinois, about five miles from our house. My wife and I had gone there earlier that week for a Christmas party, and we both thought it was nice that everybody in the neighborhood had decorated their homes. However, rather than drive through Sycamore to the subdivision as I had done with my wife, I decided to save time by taking the back roads. It turned out to be a bad choice.

We saw a few decorations at farmsteads en route, and when we got a little north of Sycamore, I turned down a road that I thought would lead to the subdivision. I was wrong. We drove around for half an hour without seeing any lights at all, let alone Christmas lights. However, while we were lost, we had a very interesting conversation:

"Daddy," Kathleen asked, "Do you believe in Santa?"

"Do you?" I asked.

"Yes," she said.

"Then I do, too," I said.

My answer seemed to be acceptable. Score one for Daddy. Soon came another question.

"Do you believe in God?" she asked.

This one caught me off guard. I'm sorry to say despite attending St. Elizabeth Elementary School and serving as an altar boy, and despite a higher education that included exposure to Hinduism, Buddhism, existential philosophy and the theological writings of Paul Tillich, I was not prepared to give my daughter a definitive answer at that moment. I had never been able to assimilate any of the things I learned into a set of beliefs that made much sense to me, and it seemed to me that an appropriate answer would require a lengthy discussion of abstract and complex theological and philosophical thought. And after all that, it still pretty much comes down to a leap of faith. The thought of trying to explain all of this to my daughter in a few simple words seemed overwhelming. However, in all my feeble reflections on the subject of religion and God, Being and Non-Being, I have come to one conclusion: I do not believe that there is nothing—which implies I must believe that there is something. And so, I took a leap that night and provided my daughter with a slightly boiled-down version of what would otherwise have been a very lengthy and probably confusing answer.

"Yes," I said.

Her response: "I do, too."

There was a short pause, then: "Daddy, do you believe in heaven?"

I thought for a moment. "I believe we will always be together," I said.

"I think Pop is in heaven," said Kathleen.

Pop was my mother-in-law's father—Kathleen's great grandfather. He had died earlier that year after a long illness.

"It made Grandma sad when Pop died," she continued.

"Yes, it did," I said.

"I know what Grandma's mom's name was," she said. "It was Gram."

"That's right," I said.

"I liked Pop," said Kathleen. Then she added, "It's not nice to make fun of old people."

"No, it's not."

There was another short pause.

"Everybody dies, even if they don't think they will," said Kathleen.

There was no skirting this comment. "That's true," I said.

We drove along the blacktop highway, cutting across the countryside. I hadn't noticed it until then, but at some point it had started to snow—big, heavy, wet flakes. Other than that, it was a very still, dark December night. My daughter was quiet for a long time, but she was alert, looking out the window, thinking hard. Finally, she spoke again.

"I'm a little bit afraid of dying," said Kathleen.

Fear of dying...at last, a subject that I knew something about.

"A lot of people are afraid of dying," I said, "because we don't know what it's going to be like."

"Yeah, we don't know what it's going to be like in the ground or if we'll go to heaven," she said.

I did not want her to have nightmares about being in the ground. "You don't actually go in the ground," I told her. "Your body does, but by then you've left your body."

She thought about this, then said, "I don't get you."

"That's okay," I said. "Wherever you go, I'll be there." This I truly believed. I could not imagine any circumstances, even death, that would cause me to drift very far from my daughter.

"And Pop will be there," said Kathleen. "And Gram."

"That's right."

The conversation went on like that for a while longer. I was a little angry with myself for not being more prepared for such a conversation, but I was pleased to see that her mind was already at work on some of life's biggest questions. I took comfort in the realization that my daughter would probably be able to figure out most things for herself—which means she'll be a lot better off in the long run than she would be if she relied on someone like her father to figure things out for her.

While all this was going on, I was still not finding the neighborhood. At some point I realized that Kathleen didn't really know why we were driving around. When I said we were going "to look at Christmas lights," she thought I meant that we were going to a store to buy more lights for the Christmas tree. By the time she figured out the real purpose of our trip, she was pretty tired. When I finally found the neighborhood, she was asleep.

It was just as well. On second glance, the decorations in the neighborhood seemed ordinary and unimaginative. There was nothing particularly wonderful or awe-inspiring about them. I drove around for a little while, but by then I was tired, too, so I turned around and headed home.

The whole excursion could have been pretty depressing. I had wanted to show my daughter some wonderful Christmas lights. Instead, I got lost. Then, when I finally found the neighborhood, the lights were nothing special. It was a far cry from the memories I had of driving around, looking at decorations when I was a kid.

But that's okay. We had discussed Santa and God and heaven and death—a conversation I would not soon forget. And at the end of the evening, I was heading home while my daughter slept like an angel in the seat next to me. I would not trade that drive with my daughter for anything.

Just then, Kathleen opened her eyes a little.

"Daddy?" she asked.

"Yes?" I answered. She didn't answer right away. I looked over at her. She looked very warm and cozy—very peaceful—the way a child in warm pajamas and a blanket should look when out for a Christmas drive with her father.

"Yes," I repeated softly. "What is it?"

"Maybe this is heaven," she said.

I thought about that for a moment.

"Yes," I said. "Maybe it is."

Mike O'Mary is Founding Dreamer of dreamofthings.com, and a writer of essays, fiction, drama and sketch comedy. He has published stories and essays in numerous periodicals, and he has written and produced sketch comedy in Chicago. He was also a commentator on WNIJ - Northern Illinois Public Radio, doing weekly commentaries as part of the local segment of National Public Radio's *Morning Edition* program.

In addition to his creative work, Mike has more than 20 years of experience writing speeches, annual reports and other executive communications for many leading corporations.

Mike is a graduate of Knox College (BA in Economics and English-Writing), the University of Montana (MFA in Creative Writing, MA in English Literature), and the Second City Comedy Writing Program.

For more information, visit dreamofthings.com

Made in the USA
Lexington, KY
29 November 2012